MESMERIZINGLY SADLY BEAUTIFUL

Michael –

With love &
gratitude &
Jinspiration

Also by Matthew Lippman

The New Year of Yellow

Monkey Bars

American Chew

A Little Gut Magic

MESMERIZINGLY SADLY BEAUTIFUL

Matthew Lippman

Four Way Books
Tribeca

For Michael

Library of Congress Cataloging-in-Publication Data

Names: Lippman, Matthew, 1965- author.
Title: Mesmerizingly sadly beautiful / Matthew Lippman.
Description: Tribeca : Four Way Books, [2020]
Identifiers: LCCN 2019031738 | ISBN 9781945588488 (trade paperback)
Classification: LCC PS3612.I647 A6 2020 | DDC 811/.6--dc23
LC record available at https://lccn.loc.gov/2019031738

This book is manufactured in the United States of America and printed on acid-free
paper.

Four Way Books is a not-for-profit literary press. We are grateful for the assistance
we receive from individual donors, public arts agencies, and private foundations.

Funding for this book was provided in part by a generous donation
in memory of John J. Wilson.

PROUD MEMBER

[clmp]

We are a proud member of the Community of Literary Magazines and Presses.

CONTENTS

PART 1

PART 2

PART 3

PART 1

IF YOU DON'T WANT YOUR KIDS TO HAVE SEX DON'T FINISH THE BASEMENT

This guy, Lev, at the dinner party said,
If you don't want your kids to have sex, don't finish the basement.
I don't remember anything anymore, my fifty-two-year-old brain a
soggy piece of kale,
but I remembered what Lev said.
It's because Lev is the heart in *levov*
where all the stories come from.
Here's the story: we were eating the salmon and he was talking about
his kids,
all grown up,
and my kids were in the basement playing ping pong,
not yet thirteen.
There was beer and wine and gluten-free challah and gluten-free Tiramisu
and the walls were red and gluten-free.
That's the whole story.
The other story is that when a guy says something like that
you have to remember where you were when you first had sex.
It could have been in a car, in an attic, between two trees, under the moon,
near the factory, inside the deep blue sea, in the onion patch.
Sex is an onion.
It's translucent and sweet and will make you cry your face off.
It's a swimming pool on fire and a gorilla who knows how to speak
seven languages.
If you are lucky enough to have sex in a finished basement,

this is a good thing.

If you have sex in an unfinished basement, not so good—all that dust,

those exposed water heaters, boilers, and rusted rakes.

So when Lev said,

If you don't want your kids to have sex, don't finish the basement,

I took a bite of my salmon and here's the last part of the story.

My kids are going to grow up and have sex.

A sad and wide-eyed, ecstatic sex, if they're lucky,

and so I left the table in the dark middle of winter to finish the basement—

buy some rugs, some cheap pillows, and a jukebox,

one of those old school Wurlitzers with the automatic eye.

Fill it up with all the songs that make your heart burst, I will tell them.

Play your music

till the needle runs those records bare bone beauty and glisten.

SOMEONE WILL LOVE YOU MANY TIMES

Someone will love you many times.

Many times over and over a red flame.

Over a million dollars and someone will love you a million dollars.

You will be loved from all over and from pockets and sandwiches

and someone will stick her hand through a plate-glass window to love you

and from between two sheets.

Over and over and many times love will come at you

from a rooftop with billowy sheets

and Miley Cyrus will love you

and so will Spiro Agnew. Many times

the Earth will love your stomach,

for many times and for the thousands of times you have answered the door

and no one was there.

For the many times you were down on your knees between the tile and

the toilet.

Someone will take your hair and hold it behind your head

many, many times over and over.

Someone will walk with you down the summer path,

all those pink and purple wildflowers getting wild for you,

getting wild for your love and for the stench of your absence.

You will send it back time and time again—

when the buildings shake, when the show is over,

when the shadows creep tall into your tall brain and mess it up.

It is a truth that can't be untruthed—

that someone will love you many times no matter how tired they are,
the way a blade of grass takes itself not too seriously
and grinds out other blades of grass. Look at them out there,
all stupid and green
in the backyard,
count them all. I bet you can't.
That's how many times you will be loved, count them all,
I bet you can't.
By someone who couldn't be more serious about love.
And is.

HOURS AND HOURS OF GRASS

We buy all this food.
Thousands of acres of grapes and rolled oats before they are rolled.
We buy the banks of the Mississippi and the tundra between one Serengeti
and another Mojave.
Sometimes, on a whim,
I go out and get a shopping cart of bones and water.
The kids can't get enough.
They eat and sing and fart and blow.
It's endless.
That's the one thing about being a parent
that no one every mentions. Massive consumption.
An endless loop of Western Civilization,
of American thievery and piggery.
Twelve acres of Ho-Hos.
Thirteen thousand bottles of Twitter tweets.
I am sure there are kids in other worlds
that could not conceive of the barrel of stuff, which lives in the front yard.
I want to go there. Wherever there is.
With my kids.
Sit them down inside a stone building and say look:
There's one dinosaur in the corner. That's it.
Her name is Françoise
and then there is the grass.
Hours and hours of grass, right outside.

Go to it.

Be in it.

Soft and quiet and wild.

Make boats and computers and oceans and blankets.

Then, when you come home hungry and tired

we will eat the same chicken and dates,

those and figs and moonbeams,

and that will be everything.

No joke.

It will be all you get.

THE OCEAN IS A FLOWER CALLLED ROBERTO CLEMENTE

Roberto Clemente kicked my ass last night.
He came out of the darkness like a train whistle
with his 21 Pittsburgh jersey tucked in
and laid me out with a left hook.

I fell to the grass and screamed,
What's your problem, Roberto?
Couldn't sleep, he said.
Get a motel.
He said, My plane crashed. I am dead.
Go home.
He said, I come from Carolina, Puerto Rico.
So, what's the problem?
He said, My name is Roberto.
I have three sons and three thousand base hits.
My name is Roberto Clemente.

And when his plane took off from San Juan,
overloaded with bananas and gauze
for the earthquake victims of Managua,
it was New Year's Eve
and his eyes were bloodshot bullets
under the canopy of the Atlantic Ocean.

When the sharks got their teeth into him,
the turtles,
the manatees and sting rays,
the vapor trail of his gait around second base
brushed back the wind.

Ten hours later my father woke me to say, El Padré, Roberto,
no longer swings for the fences.
I was seven.
I have been seven ever since.

STILL STILL STILL

It's enough to sit down in the middle of the street,
the garbage trucks picking up trash,
the school buses stopping and starting,
the dirty rain falling from the neon clouds;

it's enough to make you collapse in the middle of a speech you are
giving on human rights
or animal rights
or the right of the Earth to be as clean as it was 10,000 years ago;
enough to make you put down the pen, the gavel, the scalpel,
the international phone call,
and get on a bike and bike, hard,
to your child's school, walk into her classroom,
and hold her tight
without apologizing to the teacher for your interruption;

it's enough to toss the phone into the river, the computer into the lava pit,
turn to the person next to you
and offer them your hand, eye, maybe even a lung.

I'm saying I'm tired. We are all tired.

All around everyone is doing the best that they can do.
He makes the best pot roast,

11

she crafts the tallest building,
the bagel people whip up the best bagels,
the lovers love,
the students write the smartest papers on governmental corruption
as humanly possible and still, still, still,

there is someone outside the room with a backhoe
filled with battered Clorox bottles,
steel-tipped bullets, and vice grips ready to tear apart hearts.

It's enough to take your feelings and slide them onto a towel,
all of your feelings, all of your human and animal feelings,
jam them into a towel,
all of your decency and rage and joy and bullshit and horror and
excitement,
walk out into the street and into the mountain, the cave and the field,
and wrap up any live thing you can find in that soft cloth,
the whole world of live things,
to turn back that backhoe,
push it away into some place in the imagination
that won't even let us imagine it anymore.

THE SAVING

We save our children.

Some days we save them from the riptide and the masked gunman on
the bleachers,

the armed robber under the stairs,

we save them. We save them

from the spiders in their dreams

that breathe fire

and then we walk on that fire

to get them away from the burning buildings, raging.

We look at our children and we save them with meanness in our eyes

and the eventual moment when all patience is lost

and they tell us to *go fuck ourselves,*

we'd never understand what is in their hearts, anyway.

Sometimes, we think they save us, and they do,

from the lies we tell ourselves about how special our lives have been—

flying in the circus, the boardroom, at the operating table,

the gas pump.

But, really, it is we who save them

from the car smash-ups in snowstorms and their loneliness

when it backs up on their bodies like monster waves

smashing down without warning.

We save *them.*

Then, when all is said and done,

when we think all the saving has been used up,

when the Saving Shop has been closed down for the night,

we get a note from our old high school friend,

Sad news, my father passed peacefully in his sleep, service Monday,

so we go down to the kitchen and make herb-encrusted chicken, potatoes,

and garlic-infused broccoli

for the grieving.

It does not matter that we want some saving too,

that we want our beloved, our neighbor,

the bear in the woods,

to wrap woolly arms around us in the naked night

and hold us so close it hurts—

we are in the business of saving.

It's an endless and priceless monotony

that does not ever finish—

the way we save,

the day-to-day saving,

the way we take our hands and put them out and say, *Bleed, it's alright,*

I will catch you in your breaking.

THE INFINITE JOKE OF A FREEZING RAIN OF SHUTTLECOCKS

It doesn't matter how much Van Morrison you listen to,
how many Museum of Fine Arts that you visit,
the shuttlecock of time comes down extraordinarily fast
and smashes you to pieces.

There was that time in Sag Harbor when we played badminton for hours
after a day at Windmill Beach.
The hot sweat, the cold Labatts.
That shuttlecock rifled its little plastic nub at us
but we had no idea that this would be the way of things.
Our children birthed, our parents on the way out.
Some days we'd put on *Veedon Fleece* to slow it down
but all of a sudden the kids were sixteen and kinda drunk.
We went to the Richter exhibit,
the Rothko retrospective—didn't matter,
one mother slipped into dementia,
another father dead in the ground.

We ran to our record collections with our museum memberships
and threw *Moondance* at Monet,
Common One at Caravaggio.
Nothing helped.
The shuttlecock slammed into our faces saying, "Listen to us, listen up."
And we did, the welts growing wider and faster, bumpier and pink.

15

Time just marched on.
The body began to sag in weird places—under the tongue,
between the ribs—
and then one day we woke and couldn't drink beer anymore,
get those greasy fries from The Frye Shoppe.

Tonight, alone in our rocking chairs beneath a frozen moon,
we raided the radio for "Brown Eyed Girl," for "Hyndford Street,"
and found both.
We turned up the dial to ten and walked outside.
But it was too late.
We had lost to the infinite joke of a freezing rain of shuttlecocks
that drove us back into our small rooms and stained white walls
littered with the posters of Picasso and Murray,
Hockney and Hopper,
and that one original Miro
hidden beneath the floorboards

so when the thieves came
there'd be something left.

I WISH

Tony Hoagland wrote a poem called "Dickhead."
I wonder how many poems will be written entitled "Shithole?"
How a word becomes more than a word
is a terrible thing sometimes.
Last night, watching the football game,
my friend's daughter, Orly, came downstairs
and handed us *The New Yorker.*
She is ten.
There was a picture of the president in a onesie
sucking on a pacifier.
She said, *Makes me gross.*
Her father said, *Shithole,* really loud.
She smiled, and said *Shithole* back.
That's what happens now.
Across the country
ten-year-old kids wear baseball caps
with the word *Shithole* on the rim
and if you imagine it long and hard enough
it becomes the country of your body
which is a terrible thing.
A terrible, horrible thing.
I miss Tony Hoagland.
I miss his poem.
His poem is about the high school locker room

and jock straps
and other boys saying nasty things
and owning words
and turning words into sunflowers
when they have been bricks of coal
hurled at other people's heads.
It makes me sad and the sadness takes over
when my friends' ten-year-old daughter goes up to bed
and takes that word with her
instead of a book on rare gems,
or a cassette player with a mixed tape
her mother made for her
of all the cool songs from 1976,
the first one "I Wish."
I wish Stevie Wonder, Tony Hoagland, and Orly,
could sit down for dinner one night
adorned in long Technicolor robes,
laughing so hard that the sound of their laughter
eradicated the word *Shithead* from the lexicon,
erased it so thoroughly that there would be no more cartoons of him
in his infant clothes,
sucking his thumb,
watching television clips of himself into oblivion.

HUMAN SNOWBLOWER

So what that Dave Letterman's got a big white beard,

I'm the human snowblower.

That's what my neighbor from Alabama said to me the other night.

He said, "You're a goddamn human snowblower,"

and, seriously, it was the nicest thing anyone has said to me in decades.

It was five degrees outside and I said, "Roll Tide."

He said, "I'm an Auburn fan."

I said, "Sucks for you," but really, I don't know a damn thing

about the NC double A gridiron.

I just know that I don't care about Dave Letterman's new Netflix series.

Frankly, I think he looks goofy with that big, white beard.

I want to write his PR people and ask them if he'll have me on his next

TV special,

the one where he has a stubble-free face;

have me on to talk about the poetry of Erika Meitner;

have me on to roll eggs stuffed with firecrackers down granite steps;

have me on to chat about what it's like

to be a human snowblower

and I'll say, "Bring me up to Connecticut the next time it blizzards

and I'll whistle clean your driveway in no time."

But then I realize all my fantasies are pathological.

I don't want to be Dave's entertainment flunky

like that guy Rupert the deli dude.

That was an exercise in:

Hey, let's use the Indo-Asian guy to boost ratings.
Or not?
What do I know?
We are all good inside,
I'm sure of that.
My neighbor from Alabama knows that, too.
He's done two tours in Afghanistan, shot some people in the face,
and the last time he got back from that part of the world asked me
if I'd let his rescue dog crap on my lawn
because we have some green space in the backyard and he doesn't.
Swear to god, he said,
We'll clean up after she poops.
I'm out here blowing snow for hours with my thirty-horsepower shovel
and all I want to do is go inside to my living room
and have my own talk show,

Ladies and Gentleman, David Letterman
and his goofy-ass beard.

GLORIOUS AND BORED

Today I looked at people.
It was like looking at the green and scratched earth.
I felt so sad and bored.
I sat at the counter of Dunkin Donuts
and waited for my broken car to be fixed
by the mechanic across the street.
People in big coats came in for coffee and chocolate-covered donuts.
All day long it was a donut-and-coffee fest.
I drank my tea and did not have any memories.
It was glorious and beautiful
and the people were glorious and beautiful.
From sunup to dinnertime everyone was so happy in their big furs and
rusty boots
at the Dunkin Donuts.
I did not know what to do with myself in the sadness and boredom.
I did not eat or talk on the phone or play the flute.
It's hard to look at people these days.
We don't pay enough attention to other people's faces.
The way they contort into rivers.
The way they mutate into cities
and yearn for other faces that are rivers and volcanoes.
Look up. Look at me
so I can look at you.
That's all anyone wants to say

but we are all too busy being glorious and bored.
I want to believe otherwise.
My car is still not ready
and I am at the orange counter.
I have been here my whole life.
My tea is cold.
I have been here all day.
It's cold outside and the donuts are all gone.
I'm sure they were bad for everyone
but tasted so great.
I love your face.
It is a beautiful face.

PART 2

STRIKE A VOGUE

I am thinking about Mimi O'Donnell today,
how Philip Seymour Hoffman just up and split,
put a needle into his thigh one too many times,
and everyone said *Addiction is a disease.*
I get that, I do, but, Philip,
if you are out on the tundra
and all the mad, wild-eyed hyenas are coming for your babies,
do you choose the spear
or the dope?
I'm thinking, Dude,
you gotta pick up the spear
no matter how screwed up your need is,
no brainer.

Hell, I loved him in *Boogie Nights* and that crazy indie film he did with
Marisa Tomei
but this morning I am thinking about Mimi and her children
and the little article in *Vogue*
and wondering how everything got so public
and isn't that some weird-ass kind of addiction, too.
I mean if my wife put a needle in her arm
and never came back
and she was some famous Dalai Lama enlightened-mind superstar,

I'm not having *Vogue* come over to my house to ask questions
about how our cat is getting along.

I'm thinking about Mimi O'Donnell today.
I can see her quiet
and her kids and their dog and refrigerator with orange-juice stains
on the second shelf.
It is stupid that I read the article in *Vogue*
and it is stupid that Phil left his kids.
It makes me mad that he couldn't pick up the spear instead of the needle,
run wild at those wolves
and like Wonder Woman,
jump off some huge stone or building
and cut the heart out of those wanna-eat-your-children-beasts.
I bet if Gal Gadot had to choose between the needle and the spear,
Wonder Woman or not,
you'd know where to put your money.

I'm thinking of Mimi O'Donnell this morning.
The sun is blazing through the bare trees
and then I'm not thinking about her anymore.
I'm thinking about her kids.
I'm thinking about my kids, downstairs, asleep,
and my bloody hands, stained with the blood of a thousand wild dogs.

You know those beasts,
your tundra is filled with them too,
the crows circling to feed,
the lions feeding,
your kids knowing good and damn well
that when they wake up
you'll be in the kitchen making the peanut butter and jelly sandwiches
for lunch
no matter how sick you are,
no matter what the disease.

MEAT GRINDER

There's a meat grinder in the classroom
that two students used
to make an artistic representation of race
as social construct
for their *Museum Room in America* project.
That was their thing—race as social construct.
Take a big ball of meat, that's humanity,
everyone the same—fat, oil, protein—
then shove it into the bowl at top,
turn the crank,
and what comes out the bottom end
goes this way and that.
Black, Irish, Italian, White, Muslim.
You get the picture.

The meat grinder sits on a desk across the room.
Some days, kids come in and mess with it.
They unscrew the crank.
They bolt it to the desk.
It just stays there, gets moved around, sings, farts,
holds itself tight
when all the lights have been turned off
and the radiator clanks.
Right now, it sits alone on the tabletop

and there is Duduk music coming out of my speakers.

It makes the meat grinder sad.

Once, a wild band of Turks ran through an Armenian village

and wiped everyone out.

The meat grinder knows it had something to do with this.

That it was not the hand that shredded the ball of beef.

That it was the tool.

One day the students will come into this room and dismantle the meat grinder

to its elemental parts.

They will leave. Go home to their neighborhoods

and their dogs and families.

All the lights will get shut down and the radiators will clank.

When they come back in the morning

the meat grinder will be fashioned back to its whole self.

Like magic had something to do with it.

Like a force greater than ourselves

will always know something we never could.

AND YOU MOANED A LITTLE MOAN

One day you're going to die.
You are going to get up in the morning and you are not going to live
anymore.
Maybe you will be in the bathroom looking at the left side of your face,
remembering when your first love kissed you right there
under the eye
while she held on to the side of the bed
and you moaned a little moan so soft
she did not hear
but you knew it was a flower
and so you were happy.

You might be in the hospital bed hooked up to all those machines with
your children around you,
the young one bored out of her mind
like she couldn't be bothered with your death,
her meeting too important downtown
at the fancy restaurant, Laurent,
but you know she loves you
and so it does not matter that the clouds slowly dissolve into pink.

You might be looking at the crab apple tree out the back window
while the deer stands on its hind legs to get a taste
or you might be jerking off

or falling asleep

or just crossing the street with your friend

when the father of the girl you go to school with is in a rush,

in his car,

on his phone,

his eyes somewhere else

and he smashes into you

and that's it.

I have a friend—-his brother is dying.

It means nothing.

It means everything.

It is the world.

It is not the world.

I wonder if death is just an inconvenience?

When my grandmother died, it was.

I was on my way to the pharmacy to get toothpaste and she died

so I had to go to her apartment.

She was lying there on the couch, ashen,

wrapped in an afghan.

I was sad.

I was annoyed.

I need to say I am sorry to her but she has been dead for ten years.

Will my children be inconvenienced when I die?
I must be a cold person.
Have I raised cold children?

One day you are going to die.
I will come to your funeral and miss you.
I will cry.
When it is over,
I will go to the store and buy Brillo Pads for tomorrow night's greasy
dishes.
It is important.
Nothing is important
and the soft tissue is everything.

THE WHEEZE IN THE WINE THE MALT IN THE MIX

I have lived a highly unexceptional life.
There are no visits to Manchester United.
No conversations in Mandarin
with overseas business partners on international trade.
Certainly not any high-end bottles of whisky in the basement
to proclaim any sort of vision.
I have lived a life on the couch
with my feet inside a sandbox
watching the Knicks.
I hate the Knicks
but the couch is transportation of the optimum speed for me.
A couch on the sidewalk
thrown out by college kids headed for international trade MBAs at UPenn
who will ride the big ships
is perfect.
It could stink of bad beer and bongs,
I'm not getting on that train to France,
that gondola from the Bronx to Bologna.
I'm not going to the moon or Soweto, or to build new homes in San Juan
for those who lost theirs in Maria.
No. I would rather just sit here
and listen to icy rain pellets
hit against panes of glass
that have not been cleaned in years.

I am profoundly unexceptional.

The wheeze in the whine. The malt in the mix. The memory in the DNA.

It took fifty-three years to get here and I'm glad just to tell the truth.

The wind is cold in January on Martha's Vineyard.

Jim Hall plays a mean guitar.

All the plastic in the world will eventually lead to the end
of the bees.

THE AGE OF THE BULLET

Forget the Age of Enlightenment. The Industrial Age.
This is the Age of the Bullet.
One flew past my window this morning, tore through a watermelon.
The beauty of blowing up a watermelon with a bullet
is that it mirrors blowing up a body
with a bullet.
The water weight is equal or equivalent.
The bullet.
There goes another one, sliding across the ice skating rink.
When it hits the back of the net,
the red light will flash, the horn will sound,
and everyone will jump from their seats in ecstatic fury.
Beer will fly.
Little children will fly.
The home team will have won.
These days bullets sprout other bullets in the bullet garden.
One is torn from its stem and rips through the face of J's friend
the day before graduation.
The day before graduation
J and his friends celebrate with beer and brats.
The moon is out. It's June. It's J's day
until a purple and gold bullet
breaks through the back of his friend's cheek.
No matter how enlightened an age

the bullet trumps mindfulness.

When J saw his friend

brain-bits and blood,

there were shadows that looked like darkness

coming through the trees.

J ducked.

He thought it was the shape of a bullet coming for him next.

It was shadows.

They looked like bullets,

like flowers,

the pretty pink ones that taste like watermelon and metal

and J's on the ground, over his friend's face

cursing the Lord's Prayer to anyone who will listen.

A FIRST TRUE LOVE BIG PROBLEM

My problem is that I think every conversation is filled with love and the
big heart.
It's the same thing that happens to me
when I stand near a tree or open a pint of Rum Raisin.
It becomes everything and I love it.
If we talk about Jesus or hamburgers
it's a love story
even though I don't believe in genuflecting
and cook a mean medium rare on the open grill.

My problem is that when I stand with you, near you,
and we talk about the bad political situation
it's like you are telling me that every wind you have ever felt
you felt with me,
every log cabin you ever built,
you built with me.
This means we got bloody and sweaty together.
It means we had *something* beautiful and dirty, together.
So, when we talk about getting the gutters cleaned
or how cool that cloud is next to the window
looking to get inside
we are bloody and sweaty together.

My problem is that this happens the first time we talk, ever,
in the histories of our lives,
in the body electric gone berserk.

It's a true love problem.
It's a first true love big problem
and there is nothing I can do about it.
It's how my lungs and blood and bad eyesight and overweight snoring
all fit in together.
Excuse me then if I want something back from you in that moment
when we share a table at Starbucks,
and have words about what bus you might need to take to get
downtown to the opera house.
It is not fair. It is not right of me. I know it, but
I have a problem.
It's a first love into a lonely love
last love problem.
There's too much of it in my heart
and I want everyone to have it, all of us.
That's my problem. It's huge.
It gets me in so much trouble.
Do you feel it?
Forgive me if I want you to have it, too.

REVOLUTIONARY SEXUALITY

When the ladies in the hallway come out of the loo
talking about Al Franken
a bird lands inside my mind.
I want it to stick around.
Call it Ed.
Have a beer with it on a rock wall somewhere in Western Mass.,
Bluff Street, where my family owned a cabin in the middle of nowhere.
It was so big the thing had no running water, electricity, heat—
just how my folks wanted it.
They were drunk liberals who thought landscape
was more important than cash
and this is where I want to go with Ed,
crack a Goose Island dark brew,
talk sonnets, football, recipes from the old country
that involve pestles and mortar.

When the women come out of the loo one says *Al*
and the other says *Franken*.
Ed lands on my cerebral cortex.
I reach out my fingers.
He reaches out his feathers
and we are in Western Mass.
on a rock wall.
It's close to winter but not yet winter.

The stone under our butts is cold
and we can feel the whole history of revolution in our ass cheeks.
It burns and is soft all at once.
We are sad because we know deep in our bird breasts
that we had nothing to do with any of it
and are lucky to have found one another.
Slowly we get drunk, but not the belligerent kind of boozy.
Something quieter, slower,
that will eventually make us lie down with one another in the stinky soil,
on top of dead leaves,
and fall asleep to a tenderness we've made perfectly
out of not touching.

BODIES ARE THINGS TO RESCUE THEMSELVES

My body is not a skateboard.
It is not the Emancipation Proclamation.
The sun tenderizes my hands. They wrinkle.
They shine.
My body is not the Golden Gate Bridge.
It is not a Wurlitzer at the fingertips of Bernie Worrell.
I sit in the sun and it bakes my face off.
I am tired of women getting punished for being women.
My body is not a fallen tree.
It is not Toni Morrison or the neighbor who fights fires
and rides the backs of ambulances
to save the day.
My lord is not my body
and my body is not my lord.
It is a sense of self in the sunshine.
When my daughter caught her body falling down the stairs
she stopped it.
Bodies are things to rescue themselves
and other bodies next to them.
This is the reason for arms and lungs
and all the other parts that go chug and chime.
I realized this in the body of Newman Street
when I was so fully inside of my body,
I was outside of my skin.

We have them to stop pain even in the destruction of those around us.

My body hurts in the sun.

The knees spit.

The elbows ricochet off bone and spur.

When the phlegm comes up

the whole throat is a broken piece of beef.

When the bird's body was going to die in the crawlspace

I crawled into the crawlspace to let it free.

It speared my cheek with its beak but I held it.

Then I let its body go and it was gone.

My back hurt for days.

In the sun I can still feel that hurt.

It goes back centuries.

The Romans. The Spanish Inquisition,

the slave owner and his whip against the back of the black man's neck.

In the sun my body feels nice.

It percolates.

It is warm and reaches out across San Francisco Bay

to feel the body of San Anselmo.

It puts its arms across the jungle and gets its hands sliced off.

I am are to help, it says in the sunshine;

in the sunshine

the body emulates the sunshine.

JOY RIDE

We think we own this world.
The clouds sky trees pipelines baby pandas.
So, when I saw Barry's John Deere Cobra
idling in front of the school where I don't teach physics,
I jumped into the driver's seat to defy the law of gravity.
I slammed my foot on the pedal and peeled out.
For a second I felt bad that I would piss Barry off for my joy ride
but Barry would understand.
He does not think he owns anything.
He's the guy who has seen enough shit
to know that it's the shit that owns us.
So, I drove the hell out of his Cobra,
spinning around corners like I wanted them to get the best of me,
jumping over speed bumps hoping I might take off
into the atmosphere,
really doing my best to mess with the magnetic pull of the Earth,
with the law of least resistance.
Because I was not resisting.
I was mashing my foot into the accelerator like soft sex.
Like hard sex—
making love to the world in hopes that I could get to the other side,
to the side where I no longer felt like I owned anything—a house, a
phone, a lightbulb,
my body.

Which is when I crashed into the sycamore at the end of the lane
and screamed *Barry.*
But he did not answer and I had been owned.
I had moved into one end of the tree and out the other end, right
through it,
and the world had answered. Thing is, it was no answer.
It was just the world and I was an idiot in it,
so I went back into the building and saw Barry.
He was reading a newspaper,
a story about a woman who had been half sucked out of a broken
airplane window
at 28,000 feet.
For three minutes, two men tried to pull her back in.
When she was safely in the plane
one administered CPR and one said, "I'm here."
Imagine what she saw out there, all alone,
the atmosphere smashing into her face at 268 miles an hour?
Imagine her mind and the absence of her mind.

When they interviewed the pilot of the plane
she said, "The engine exploded and I saw the angels going past me
really fast."

PART 3

MESMERIZINGLY SADLY BEAUTIFUL

(for Beth Harrison, CE)

Downtown beyond down, dude killed a coupla dudes.
Ran 'em over in a truck.
You can't make this shit up.
The Hudson River put its face into the sunset and screamed.

My wife comes upstairs.
I'm on the floor spread out like some half-dead bison.
The cat is fat, she says.
The world is too hard, she says.
Our children will inherit a planet we could not have imagined, she says.
I have already imagined it but I don't tell her.

The Hudson River put its face into a sunset and screamed.
It wanted to pull the life of the dead back from the dead.
You can't imagine what it has seen.

Downtown beyond down
people stood with candles in a human candelabra
but the light could not bring the dead back.
It was a light thrown back by snow.
What is snow so far away snow?
It's the same as asking

what is a fog horn so far away
that sounds in fog?

It's out there in the harbor beyond the downtown down of the Hudson.
This river that slips its cheeks into the sunset and screams.
Screams its bloody head off.
Enough is sure enough
and those people on bicycles.
They light the shadow in death.
The human candelabra shadow of dying.

When we sit down on the sidewalk in the light
we make sure to hold one another.
I don't care what you say about this city,
we sit down together on the sidewalk
and we hold on tight.

BLOND FOR ALL THE BOYS

Frank Ocean didn't mean anything to me till Dave said check out "Self
Control"
and we sat in the hot October sun
and listened which was weird
because Dave doesn't usually hang around.
He's busy with his son and his paper route
and the gliders in his mind
that take him from one uninhabited island off the coast of India
to Friday night dinners at Joan's.
But he stayed,
sat with me and then the chorus blew over the clouds and trees,
right into us.
He said, "Just be here with this," and Frank was singing the word
summertime,
like love had won
and I looked over at Dave with his feet up on the table.
He was singing along, *summertime,* barely moving his lips,
and I thought he was going to cry.
In my mind I was saying, *Come on Dave, you can do it, you can do it,*
some weird desire in me to be in a room with another man
who cries.
You see why I am so desperately alone in this world?
Lying on two thigh-thick oak branches most days,
forty feet up,

all alone in a tree in the rain?

For a second I could feel Dave in that oak with me,

until he had to be busy again,

but for a second it was cool,

didn't matter what color Frank Ocean's hair was,

pink, green,

blond for all the boys who want to cry,

then sit up in bed,

and cry.

NATALIE WANTED TO WATCH NASCAR

Natalie wanted to watch NASCAR
I said *Hold up* not my thing
we were on the attic floor
cleaning up gel markers and Monopoly houses
Come on Dad don't go to the basketball
the Cavs were playing the Pacers
and Lebron was doing wizard shit
but Natalie wanted Talladega
so I let it go
and there were fighter jets flying over the race track
and Kyle Busch had his neck in sweats
the national anthem stung like a dinosaur tooth in the thigh
she wanted to watch a perfect blue sky drip into a big green engine
and the green infield with Budweiser tall boys
all those good ol'-looking lads
Davey Allison and Joey Logano
it's an America we don't know
but maybe we should
maybe all of us Pete Seeger northern liberals
need to get down to Alabama on a hot Sunday in late April
embrace the Bible and crocodile boots
to see how it feels,
to see how it feels to lean a bit more to the right,
I'm just saying to be on the other side of the infield

to be closer to what we don't know than ever before

to pour wiper fluid into beer mugs with strange bedfellows

and get smashed drunk on piston grease

so our tires get bigger

hug the tarmac tighter

I know it was the fast cars and sleek women that had Natalie

feeling the NASCAR wizard magic

and you could smell the oil and gasoline

on the camera glass when Jimmie Johnson's vehicle

slid into William Byron on turn three that started a fourteen-car smash up

she liked that

we all like that

especially when no one gets hurt

WAR IS NOT HEALTHY FOR CHILDREN AND OTHER LIVING THINGS

Aliza said she found the poster in her parents' basement or attic
and had it framed.
It is water-damaged, I could see the brown stains
that reminded me of the brown stains
that fly across the sky and the country
and the playground and the face of the guy next door
with all the rifles.
We had that poster, too, in our apartment in 1970 and 1974
and '80 and '86,
carried it around to remind us what needn't be reminded.
I don't know when my parents got rid of it but it never left.
When I was a kid we all wore the button on our jean jackets
even when we fell off the monkey bars and the pin rammed into our chests
like we knew something and we did.
We didn't care; we were that kind of kid.
We wanted to do something important, be important,
show the world that Orange Crush was the joint soda
and Wacky Packs and Marvin Gaye were the joint soda
and we meant something.
We did and when I saw the poster in the frame on Aliza and Daniel's wall
I was upset that it was not on my wall for my children.
Sometimes your parents can give you something and you don't even
know it
until you know it

and then it's yours.

In 1972 it was mine,

we were children and we were other living things—

lizards and mosquitoes, we were frogs and elephants and sycamore trees.

We were our sisters and our brothers and our neighbors

and you know what, we *knew* it

because every night when we turned on the TV to watch *Rocky and Bullwinkle*

or Adam West as Batman

there was Dan Rather or Peter Jennings from Hanoi or the rice paddies of hell.

I am sad tonight

that I did not save the water-damaged poster of that flower

which my parents hung on our walls,

that sketch made by Lorraine Schneider, she died of cancer in 1972,

and I miss her.

We all miss you, Lorraine.

Our posters are stained brown now on these walls,

on the backs of our eyes like tattoos

and we give them to our children,

we say to them, here, take this flower,

it is for you.

THEY DUG UP THEIR JOY AND BURIED IT AGAIN

The kids walked out.

They walked out onto the driveway and the lawn.

They walked down the roadway and into the forest.

They found the guns and buried the guns.

They cried into their guns and the memories of their friends who had
no time.

Time to sledgehammer and time to have sex.

Time to talk against the wind and time to rest.

They walked into the forest and planted their eyes and their lips.

Dug up the ground with shovels made from guns

and planted their arms and their feet.

What else could they do?

They jumped over streams and their chests were torn up by branches
and thorns.

They did not care. They were wet.

They were naked and there were no masks.

The Estée Lauder masks and the Aztec masks.

They ripped up the earth and buried their lungs and their eyebrows.

You couldn't find a phone or a circuit board.

There were no computers or submarines.

They walked out into the forest and the forest opened up its forest arms

and welcomed them with forest spit and grime.

All the kids.

Every single kid and they buried the guns and next to the guns

they buried their fingernails and their joy.
They dug up their joy and buried it again
and their sadness anxiety
and the memories of their friends on rollercoasters
and their friends smoking dope.
They were naked and in the springtime
when the snow had melted and the sun was warm
the forest floor burst with caterpillars and ferns
and the kids walked out, back out, from the forest floor.
They were filthy and naked and
there was so much green it was blinding.

MINGUS IN THE MORNING

All morning
all I want to do
is listen to Mingus
which is probably a good sign
like the guy on the path
behind the school
taking a picture of a frog
he says something about his kid
I can't recall
earlier I recall
my cat
tried to jump out the window
through the screen
into the world
I said what's up Sammy boy
Sammy boy went wild
for the stray on our porch
who knows if he wanted to kill it
or hump it
do cats do that kind of thing
or frogs
I know Mingus did
between breakfast and the bus
maybe that's why I want to listen to his upright moan

this morning

Better Git It In Your Soul meets *Moanin'*

I want it in my balls

better yet

out beyond the roadways and factories

in the meadow where the cats and frogs frolic

it's a good sign to feel this way

that the land can still work its bass lines on my body

that the country is getting better every day

THAT IS WHY YOU HAVE TO BUY YOUR KID **ASTRAL WEEKS**

Sick and tired of the fault lines in Hawaii and California

the plants and trees and the cat at our window

sick and tired of bad Russians and crazy wife beaters

the way the moon hangs in the sky

the manager of the Walmart

all the hops and yeasts that make craft beer taste orange and pink

sick and tired of Kurt Cobain's kid

all her money

the money that I used to never have

the students in their crocodile skin luggage automobiles

sick of the Teslas and Google people telling the Apple people

buy sell reap kill maim extort defile

sick of North Koreans too

except for the one who drove his jeep to the south

got shot and can say anything he wants now about our president

his president

any president

with soup bowls of anxiety tearing up his large intestines

mostly sick and tired of anxiety

how it ruins the flora and birds

the young people who think it's cool to buy vinyl LPs

my daughter got a turntable yesterday

then I went online

I am sick of online

and bought *Astral Weeks*
it's possibly the only thing that doesn't bring me down
I hope this earth makes it
I hate feeling that I hope the earth will make it
that's why you have to buy your kid *Astral Weeks*
and hope she'll open the shrink wrap
lay down on her bed and listen to "Ballerina" a hundred times
before there's even that faint feeling
I'm tired and sick of this song
the needle used to be a forever thing inside a groove
not so much these days
look outside
dreams used to hang on the tips of flowers
you could go up to them with your whole face
suck them like bees
then return to your brothers and sisters in the hive
with so much buzzing it was honey
it was good when there was all that honey
the bees thick with themselves it didn't matter

ROE V. WADE

(for Rachel)

Yesterday my wife said she wanted to get a tattoo
we were at the beach
it was sandy
it had water and waves
my daughter rode the waves
everywhere there were seagulls
the death of humanity was everywhere
in the human throng
in the human garbage of love and beer
the tattoos were everywhere
everywhere was everywhere and we were exhausted
my other daughter said everything is so grey
in the sunshine and blue sky
every woman knew what she was talking about
I said, Babe, why do you want a tattoo
she said youth
the tight muscles of the beach were as abundant as seagulls
the deltoids and the ass cheeks
flying around
as if this was some kind of Biblical story
that part where God goes
you heathens you follower of idols

and smites the whole shit show

everywhere there were lemonade stands of ice cream and fried fish

and fried hot dogs and fried tattoos

they were burning

I hate tattoos

but when I asked Rachel where she would get hers

she pointed to her shoulder

the unexpected idea of ink on flesh

the bodies flying around the beach

the death of humanity right before us

in the car ride home

it all seemed to make more sense

my wife said

everywhere across this country women will no longer have a right to

their bodies

I could hear the anger ripping at her vocal chords

the deep heat

it was everywhere

a sunburst from the inside of her body

branding itself on the back of her shoulder

for her daughters

GRACE

I am in the playground of the kitchen.

The Brussels sprouts have their hands in the sandbox.

The garlic, pressed, slides down a Wüsthof blade.

These are my blessings.

When the neighbor complains that my tree branch is too low on her yard

I say, *Auschwitz*.

These are my blessings.

The potatoes want to roll down the slide and the hamburger gets greasy

on the monkey bars.

The broccoli slips and falls.

No stalks break and I worry

that there are too many nitrogen bombs in Nevada.

My daughter yells that there are not enough bubbles in her bath.

I scream, *Hunger*.

The porterhouse runs through the sprinkler.

It is my blessing.

When I bite it into it I am blessed.

It is the blood of the cow that is the blood of the goat

that is the blood of a ram

and we take communion.

We bow at the bima

and the Star of David

and the Star of Bethlehem
shine their lights through our eyes.
I know no other stars and the chicken swings so high on the swing
there is no more sky.

The onion gets sassy with the leek and no one wins.
They are blessed from the same acidic mother.
My wife takes issue with the way I clean the pot.
I say, *Parkland.*

When we all sit for dinner the blessings are in front of us and abundant.
We don't know them long enough
and we make sure that we get better at being born.

ACKNOWLEDGMENTS

About Place Journal, Bodega, Borderlands, Green Mountains Review, Monthly Matter, New England Review, On The Seawall, and *Plume*

THANK YOUS

I would like to thank Dorianne Laux for her support and excitement about this book.

I would like to thank Michael Morse, Alex Gould, Kevin Bolan, Adina Astor, Sharky Laguana, Naomi Laguana, Tina Cane, Michael Weissman, Pam Adelstein, Jonty Joffe, Lisa Fishbayne, Aaron Tillman, Matthew Dickman, Jay Nebel, Juan Felipe Herrera, Rebecca Lippman, Mark Heyert, David Weiss, Kerrin McCadden, Elizabeth Powell, Dave Harrity, Josh Rilla, Lisa Brown, Dave Leibowitz, Daniel DeLeon; Sally Ball;

Natalie and Eliana;

and most deeply my wife, Rachel, for everything.

Matthew Lippman's collection *Mesmerizingly Sadly Beautiful* won the Four Way Books Levis Prize in Poetry. He is the author of four other poetry collections—*A Little Gut Magic, American Chew, Monkey Bars,* and *The New Year of Yellow.* He is the editor and founder of the web-based project Love's Executive Order (www.lovesexecutiveorder.com).

Publication of this book was made possible by grants and donations. We are also grateful to those individuals who participated in our 2019 Build a Book Program. They are:

Anonymous (14), Sally Ball, Vincent Bell, Jan Bender-Zanoni, Laurel Blossom, Adam Bohannon, Lee Briccetti, Jane Martha Brox, Anthony Cappo, Carla & Steven Carlson, Andrea Cohen, Janet S. Crossen, Marjorie Deninger, Patrick Donnelly, Charles Douthat, Morgan Driscoll, Lynn Emanuel, Blas Falconer, Monica Ferrell, Joan Fishbein, Jennifer Franklin, Sarah Freligh, Helen Fremont & Donna Thagard, Ryan George, Panio Gianopoulos, Lauri Grossman, Julia Guez, Naomi Guttman & Jonathan Mead, Steven Haas, Bill & Cam Hardy, Lori Hauser, Bill Holgate, Deming Holleran, Piotr Holysz, Nathaniel Hutner, Elizabeth Jackson, Rebecca Kaiser Gibson, Dorothy Tapper Goldman, Voki Kalfayan, David Lee, Howard Levy, Owen Lewis, Jennifer Litt, Sara London & Dean Albarelli, David Long, Ralph & Mary Ann Lowen, Jacquelyn Malone, Fred Marchant, Donna Masini, Louise Mathias, Catherine McArthur, Nathan McClain, Richard McCormick, Kamilah Aisha Moon, James Moore, Beth Morris, John Murillo & Nicole Sealey, Kimberly Nunes, Rebecca Okrent, Jill Pearlman, Marcia & Chris Pelletiere, Maya Pindyck, Megan Pinto, Barbara Preminger, Kevin Prufer, Martha Rhodes, Paula Rhodes, Silvia Rosales, Linda Safyan, Peter & Jill Schireson, Jason Schneiderman, Roni & Richard Schotter, Jane Scovell, Andrew Seligsohn & Martina Anderson, Soraya Shalforoosh, Julie A. Sheehan, James Snyder & Krista Fragos, Alice St. Claire-Long, Megan Staffel, Marjorie & Lew Tesser, Boris Thomas, Pauline Uchmanowicz, Connie Voisine, Martha Webster & Robert Fuentes, Calvin Wei, Bill Wenthe, Allison Benis White, Michelle Whittaker, Rachel Wolff, and Anton Yakovlev.